Sacred Transformation Quest

Perumal Koshy

Sacred Transformation Quest
Perumal Koshy

Published by:
TDW Productions and Publishing
2023
New Delhi, India
thedigitalwordhub@gmail.com
Web: www. http://tdwpublishing.com

ISBN:
978-93-91828-44-8 (Paperback)
978-93-91828-46-2 (Hardback)

SACRED TRANSFORMATION QUEST

A set of devotional thoughts

Perumal Koshy

About the author

Dr. P. Koshy is an author, development professional and digital communication strategist. Editor Global SME News | Director at Enterprise Institute-IERD,| Writes on #SMEs, #Entrepreneurship. Former Senior Economist at World Association for SMEs/ Former Economist AMI International SAOC;
Studied at Mumbai University, NMIMS University and Birla College & KC College, Mumbai.

His books include:
Leadership in the New Normal (Edited)
SMEs and Economic Development (Edited)
Entrepreneurship & Private Enterprises in Economic Development in Rural India (Edited)
Diversity Management in SMEs
Navigating the New Normal: A Post Covid Approach for SMEs (Edited)
Micro Enterprise Development and Business Incubators
A Christmas Tale(Fiction)

Email.:caushie@gmail.com
Linkedin: https://www.linkedin.com/in/caushie

Contents

Preface

It is with great joy and humility that I present to you this collection of devotionals, "Sacred Transformation Quest," which has been a labor of love and faith spanning the years from 2009 to 2014. These devotionals are the culmination of my personal journey, reflecting connection with holy scriptures, experiences, spiritual musings, and the challenges that life often presents.

This collection comprises 18 devotionals, each grounded in the timeless wisdom of the Bible. As you journey through these pages, you will find a tapestry of thoughts, emotions, and reflections that have touched my heart and, I hope, will resonate with yours.

I did not set out to write a book when I penned these devotionals; instead, they emerged organically as responses to the ebb and flow of my spiritual life. Each devotional is a heartfelt response to the Scriptures, a meditation on the profound truths contained therein, and a testament to the transformative power of faith.

Life is a series of challenges, and it is during these moments of struggle and doubt that our faith is truly tested. The devotionals in this collection bear witness to my own trials and tribulations, and the solace I found in the words of the Bible. Through these pages, I invite you to join me in exploring how faith can be a guiding light, illuminating our path.

What you hold in your hands is not just a collection of writings but a spiritual journey. It is a quest for sacred transformation, a journey towards a deeper understanding of oneself and a closer communion with the divine. It is my hope that these devotionals will serve as a source of inspiration, comfort, and guidance for you, just as they have been for me.

As you embark on this sacred journey, I encourage you to read these devotionals with an open heart and a discerning spirit. Allow the words to resonate within you, and may they lead you closer to the source of all love, wisdom, and transformation.

Thank you for taking the time to explore "Sacred Transformation Quest." May it be a companion on your own spiritual journey, helping you navigate life's challenges and inspiring you to seek the sacred in every moment.

In faith and gratitude,
Perumal Koshy

Genesis 32:26-30 (NIV)

Then the man said, "Let me go, for it is daybreak." But Jacob replied, "I will not let you go unless you bless me." The man asked him, "What is your name?" "Jacob," he answered. Then the man said, "Your name will no longer be Jacob, but Israel, because you have struggled with God and with humans and have overcome." Jacob said, "Please tell me your name." But he replied, "Why do you ask my name?" Then he blessed him there. So Jacob called the place Peniel, saying, "It is because I saw God face to face, and yet my life was spared."

1

"I will not let you go unless you bless me!"
Genesis 32:26

Depths of Faith

This powerful declaration encapsulates a prayer of profound significance found in the Bible. It represents the heartfelt cry of a soul in crisis, seeking divine intervention. Simultaneously, it embodies unwavering faith in God's healing power to overcome adversity. Moreover, it underscores the transformative potential of a prayer for blessing.

Adversity often serves as a catalyst for the growth and development of human beings. It is during these challenging times that we recognize God's supreme authority and acknowledge our own vulnerability, leading us to implore His assistance. Remarkably, through prayer, we discover the resilience to face the obstacles before us. In numerous instances throughout the Old Testament, we encounter Jacob, a figure who wrestled with God. Notably, Jacob adamantly demanded God's blessing, proclaiming, "I will not let you go unless you bless me!" (Genesis 32:26)

Significantly, we must recognize that although God is always prepared to bless us, we often fail to ask or request His blessings as fervently as Jacob did. The moment we earnestly seek His blessings, He stands ready to bestow them upon us. Nevertheless, to make such demands, our faith must be strong, and our belief in His boundless power must be unwavering. We should cultivate a sense of ownership, acknowledging ourselves as His beloved, in order to approach Him confidently. Weak and wavering faith can never forcefully elicit His blessings. Hence, our faith in Him must be absolute.

By emphasizing the struggle for blessing, we highlight the transformative journey of faith. It elucidates the profound connection between unwavering faith, prayer, and the acquisition of God's blessings. This narrative invites us to reflect on our own struggles, reminding us that through resolute faith and heartfelt prayers, we can triumph over adversity and experience the transformative power of God's blessings in our lives.

John 21:15

In John 21, after Jesus' resurrection, he appears to his disciples by the Sea of Tiberias (also known as the Sea of Galilee). During this encounter, Jesus engages in a conversation with Simon Peter, who had previously denied knowing Jesus three times before his crucifixion.

"When they had finished eating, Jesus said to Simon Peter, 'Simon son of John, do you love me more than these?' 'Yes, Lord,' he said, 'you know that I love you.' Jesus said, 'Feed my lambs.'"

2

"Simon Son of Jonah, do you love me more than these?"
John 21: 15

Transcending Worldly Attachments

In a world consumed by material desires and ambitions, it is crucial for us to reflect upon our priorities and examine our love for Jesus Christ. Through biblical examples and the profound question posed by Jesus to Peter, we are invited to reassess our affections and embrace a love that transcends worldly possessions.

The Allure of Worldly Desires: Our lives often revolve around the pursuit of material wealth, success, and personal achievements. This insatiable appetite for more can manifest in various forms, such as money, possessions, careers, or accomplishments. However, these temporal pursuits can blind us to the true essence of love and our relationship with God.

Abraham's Unquestioning Obedience: The story of Abraham demonstrates unwavering faith and trust in God's authority. When faced with the seemingly illogical command to sacrifice his son, Isaac, Abraham did not hesitate. His love for God surpassed his attachment to worldly possessions, illustrating a deep understanding of surrendering oneself completely to God.

Jesus' Question to Peter: The poignant question asked by Jesus to Peter, "Simon Son of Jonah, do you love me more than these?" carries profound relevance for us today. It challenges us to examine our hearts and evaluate whether our love is directed towards Jesus or consumed by the world and its allurements.

Surrendering to God's Ownership: To truly love God, we must recognize that everything in our lives, including ourselves and our possessions, belongs to Him. This realization leads to a transformative surrender, allowing us to detach ourselves from worldly desires and embrace a life of true devotion.

Commitment and Detachment: The example of Sadhu Kochukunnju, a missionary preacher, highlights the significance of committing our assets, debts, and desires to the Lord. By relinquishing control and acknowledging God's ownership, we cultivate a sense of detachment from worldly possessions and align ourselves with His purpose.

Fulfilling our Duty and Mission: When our love for God is paramount, our actions take on a deeper meaning. By living for the glory of God and fulfilling our purpose in His service, life gains new depths and a profound beauty that transcends the fleeting pleasures of the world.

As we ponder the question, "Do you love Jesus?" we are challenged to reorient our affections and align them with our Creator. By prioritizing our love for God over worldly desires, we embark on a journey of surrender, detachment, and fulfillment of our divine purpose. Only through genuine love for Jesus can we experience the true richness and meaning that life has to offer.

You are the light of the world. A town built on a hill cannot be hidden. Neither do people light a lamp and put it under a bowl. Instead, they put it on its stand, and it gives light to everyone in the house. In the same way, let your light shine before others, that they may see your good deeds and glorify your Father in heaven.

Matthew 5:14-16

For you were once darkness, but now you are light in the Lord. Live as children of light.

Ephesians 5:8

3

"...so that you may become blameless and pure, children of God without fault in a warped and crooked generation. Then you will shine among them like stars in the sky as you hold firmly to the word of life."
Philippians 2:15-16

Agents of Change

As believers, we are chosen by God to make a positive impact wherever we are positioned. Regardless of the circumstances or the seeming inadequacies of our surroundings, God expects us to shine brightly and set ourselves apart.

The Promised Land, often associated with abundance and prosperity, was not necessarily endowed with abundant natural resources like its neighboring lands. However, God chose the Israelites to demonstrate that it is not the external circumstances that determine success, but their obedience and faithfulness.

Rather than shying away from the responsibility, the Israelites embraced their calling. They exemplified their uniqueness and transformed the land into a place of prosperity and abundance. Today, Israel stands as a global leader in various fields, offering solutions in bio-technology, agriculture, and farm technologies—a testament to their commitment to making a difference.Unfortunately, we often fail to recognize the potential bestowed upon us. Instead of taking ownership of our circumstances, we tend to blame God, the environment, and societal systems for our struggles. It is essential to break free from this mindset and realize that God has chosen us to bring about transformation.

Rather than fleeing from challenging situations, we should remain steadfast and determined to make a difference. God has placed us precisely where we are for a reason. By recognizing our divine purpose and potential, we can rise above the darkness and create a positive impact.

Instead of seeking escape, we must embrace our role as agents of change. Our faith calls us to be present and make a difference in every sphere of life. By relying on God's guidance and tapping into our unique gifts and abilities, we can transform our surroundings and inspire others to do the same. Let us heed the call to be present, embrace our responsibilities, and become catalysts for positive change.

For just as each of us has one body with many members, and these members do not all have the same function, so in Christ we, though many, form one body, and each member belongs to all the others.

Romans: 12: 4-5

4

And let us consider how we may spur one another on toward love and good deeds
Hebrews 10:24-25

Our Neighbours

Loneliness is a fact of life. No one has or ever will have time, for the other person and this is a reality we must come to terms with.

However, thanks to modern day gadgets like mobile phones, computers, the Internet, television, and social networking sites like Orkut, Facebook and Twitter, we are often saved from the experience of feeling lonely. They open up the world at the touch of a button, and bridge all physical distances between people.

The irony here is that because of these 'loneliness banishing phenomena', our world, even our immediate surroundings, suddenly become part of 'virtual reality'. So much so that even our neighbours become 'screen icons' and 'chat windows', and all our networking is catapulted to a space-time realm. Often our immediate physical neighbours are strangers and not the ones we interact and converse with on a daily basis or people we need to greet even.

Nurturing a 'physical' neighborhood community rarely becomes our need and priority.

My grandfather used to tell me about life till his middle age. A stark contrast from today's frenetic pace, life in his heyday was calmer, slower and had a lot more to do with what could be seen and felt rather than imagined.

In those days, there was no telephone, no electricity or even a battery powered torch. Prayer meetings used to be held in homes and were something eagerly anticipated throughout the day. All the neighbors congregated and walked together to attend such spiritual gatherings, even in the dark, with a makeshift torch made of coconut leaves. There would be three four of such leaf bunches, sufficient to keep burning till the group returned home.

Also, whenever someone needed assistance, everyone would rush to the affected person's home, and take care of the situation.But those days of glory soon passed. My grandfather laments how, with the advent of the telephone, the television and the Internet, the need to call others and meet people face to face has come down drastically. Our telephone and Internet Service Providers become our lifeline and take on the role that people in flesh and blood once performed. There is no conversation, no camaraderie and no bonding. Everything is virtual and imagined.

Today, to experience a life like that of my grandfather's, we may have to go to Amish Country, perhaps the only place where the pace of modernity is not as accelerated. Everywhere else is just a homogenous mass of modernity. Times have changed.

Sadhu Kochukunju, a missionary preacher who lived in the early part of the 20th century in the Southern part of India, brought together area prayer fellowships in his parish, and some of the neighboring parishes. The prayer fellowships in those areas, near Kozhencherry – Aranmula – Punnakkadu- Kuzhikala- etc are known as vayana groups. Vayana in Malayalam means ' 'a reading session'.

People used to come together to read and ponder upon the Bible. Apart from reading, Sadhu Kochukunju wanted that these Vayana sessions should be an opportunity for these eclectic groups of people to discuss issues in their village or neighborhood. If an individual had a problem or a need, everyone together must put their heads together and sort it out, thus becoming extended family members, he wished. So for instance, if a 'Vayana' member was arranging the wedding of his child, then the entire group should consider it a common responsibility.

But in the modern world, in the world of mobile phones, facebook, orkut and ipads, can we think of a sharing economy? Living in the spirit of sharing, caring and love is indeed the foundation for a better world and a green economy. There is no point in mindlessly embracing modernity-what is needed is take a step back and embrace some of those old habits, while imbibing the spirit of everything new. This will ensure that together in Jesus Christ, we can make this world a much better place to live.

Trust in the Lord with all your heart and lean not on your own understanding; in all your ways submit to him, and he will make your paths straight.

Proverbs 3:5-6

5

Be still, and know that I am God; I will be exalted among the nations, I will be exalted in the earth.
-Psalm 46:10

Power of Silence

At the end of a busy and chaotic day, my mind was restless, burdened by an indiscernible issue that eluded my understanding. Despite my attempts to analyze and evaluate the situation, I found myself unable to pinpoint the source of my distress. In that moment, a simple realization dawned upon me: I needed to sit in silence.

Seeking Solace in the Rain: As evening descended, heavy rain poured down, enveloping the surroundings in its rhythmic downpour. I focused my attention on the rain, absorbing its sound, the flashes of lightning, and the accompanying thunder. When the lightning and thunder grew intense, I sought shelter indoors.

The Serenity of Silence: As the rain persisted, gradually ceasing after 15 minutes, a remarkable calmness settled over the environment and within my soul. Beyond the natural symphony orchestrated by the raindrops, silence prevailed. It was in this stillness that I felt the presence of God, sensing His voice speaking to me.

The Language of Silence: In my contemplative state, I realized that God often communicates with us through silence rather than through clamor and commotion. In the absence of words and external distractions, the profoundness of His message becomes clearer. Through the silence, He guides us, offering solace and profound insights that surpass the noise of everyday life.

Embracing Divine Presence: In a world filled with constant noise and distractions, it is essential to carve out moments of silence for spiritual reflection. In these serene interludes, we can hear the whispers of God and feel His presence more acutely. The respite of silence allows us to connect with the depths of our souls, inviting divine wisdom and guidance into our lives.

Through the power of silence, we can unlock a deeper understanding of ourselves and our relationship with the divine. The rainfall served as a gentle reminder of the significance of silence in our lives, offering solace and revealing God's presence. By embracing silence, we create a space for divine communion, transcending the clamor of the world and connecting with the profound truths that reside within us. Let us cherish these moments of stillness and embrace the language of silence as a means to experience the richness of spiritual connection.

But ask the animals, and they will teach you, or the birds in the sky, and they will tell you; or speak to the earth, and it will teach you, or let the fish in the sea inform you. Which of all these does not know that the hand of the Lord has done this? In his hand is the life of every creature and the breath of all mankind.

Job 12:7-10

6

How clearly the sky reveals God's glory! How plainly it shows what He has done!

- Psalms 19:1

Sensing God's Presence

After a long and hectic day at work, my mind was greatly disturbed by an enigmatic issue. I made numerous attempts to analyze and understand the situation, but to no avail. It then occurred to me that finding solace in silence might provide the clarity I sought.

During that particular evening, heavy rain poured down relentlessly. I focused my attention on the rain, immersing myself in its sound, the flashes of lightning, the rumble of thunder, and every aspect associated with the storm. As the lightning and thunder intensified, I sought refuge indoors, seeking safety from their powerful display.

After approximately fifteen minutes, the rain subsided, leaving behind a profound sense of calmness that extended beyond the environment and penetrated my very soul. Amidst the natural melody created by the raindrops, there existed a profound silence—an utter absence of noise. In that stillness, I felt a distinct impression that God was speaking to me.

The familiar hymn, "O Lord, My God..." holds a crucial message often overlooked—the presence of God in His creation. By observing nature with a clear mind, we can sense the unmistakable presence of its divine Creator. The hymn's verses resonate deeply, reminding us of the awe-inspiring wonders that bear witness to God's power. The stars illuminating the sky, the resounding echoes of thunder, the serenade of birds in the woods, and the gentle breeze brushing against our skin—all point to the grandeur of God's creation.

In those moments of reflection, we are able to discern the sacred connection between God and His handiwork. It is through nature that God's glory is vividly displayed, reminding us of His boundless wisdom and majesty. Let us not forget the profound significance of recognizing God's presence in the world around us.

Therefore, when the weight of life's complexities burdens our minds, let us seek solace in the tranquility of nature. Just as the rain brought a cooling effect to the environment and my soul, a deliberate observation of the natural world can offer us a respite, enabling us to sense the gentle whispers of God. In the resounding silence, we discover a profound connection between our Creator and His creation, enriching our spiritual journey and nourishing our souls.

In awe and wonder, let us embrace the gift of nature as a testament to God's glory, and may it lead us to a deeper understanding of His presence in our lives.

Trust in the Lord with all your heart and lean not on your own understanding; in all your ways submit to him, and he will make your paths straight.

Proverbs 3:5-6

7

See, I am doing a new thing! Now it springs up; do you not perceive it? I am making a way in the wilderness and streams in the wasteland.

Isaiah 43:19

Self-Reinvention

Recession often serves as a catalyst for profound transitions in our lives. It forces us to embark on a soul-searching journey to examine whether our current pursuits align with our true calling and purpose.

The impact of the recession has been far-reaching, affecting individuals from various walks of life. Youngsters who were earning substantial salaries, sometimes surpassing those of their parents, found themselves without jobs. Newly married couples, middle-aged professionals, seniors, business owners, small traders, and construction workers all experienced the brunt of the crisis. Some faced complete job loss, while others had to endure significant salary reductions. Even entrepreneurs and established business owners were compelled to shutter their companies due to the economic downturn.

Coping with such a crisis is undoubtedly challenging for most individuals. Many are forced to contemplate new vocations and avenues for employment. In developing countries, the rise of the Business Process Outsourcing (BPO) industry provided high-paying jobs in the IT and BPO sectors. Mechanical engineers, civil engineers, teachers, and even doctors found themselves working in IT or IT-enabled services, earning more than they could in their respective fields. Consequently, a shortage of skilled workers emerged in non-IT sectors.

I recall a friend of mine who possessed exceptional talent in sculpting and painting. However, his educational qualifications led him to secure a highly lucrative job in the booming IT industry immediately after college. When the recession hit, he lost his job, which came as a shock to him.

For two months, he tirelessly searched for a suitable position that would offer a salary comparable to his previous earnings, or at least something close to it. Unfortunately, all his efforts were in vain. During this challenging period, he began reflecting on his passion and talent for art. He decided to dedicate himself to his craft. The art he created not only provided a potential means of livelihood but also brought him the much-needed fulfillment that had been lacking in his previous jobs.

This crisis, the current recession, serves as an eye-opener for many individuals who found themselves in sectors unrelated to their original industries. It compels them to reassess their choices, skills, and passions, urging them to consider reinventing themselves professionally.

Crises are often necessary for self-reinvention. They push us out of our comfort zones and compel us to explore new possibilities. While the initial impact may be daunting, it presents an opportunity for growth, discovery, and embracing a path that aligns more closely with our true selves.

As we navigate through these challenging times, let us embrace the potential for personal reinvention. May we use this period of crisis as a springboard for discovering our authentic vocations and creating lives that bring us not only financial stability but also a profound sense of purpose and fulfillment.

When you pass through the waters, I will be with you; and when you pass through the rivers, they will not sweep over you. When you walk through the fire, you will not be burned; the flames will not set you ablaze.

Isaiah 43:2

8

So do not fear, for I am with you; do not be dismayed, for I am your God. I will strengthen you and help you; I will uphold you with my righteous right hand.

Isaih 41:10

God's Presence in Life

In life, we often find ourselves trapped in seemingly impossible situations, with all paths sealed and no apparent way out. These are the moments when our true potential is unleashed, and we rise to the challenge with unparalleled determination.

This truth resonates with the experiences of countless migrant workers who leave their home countries behind, bidding farewell to loved ones. Despite the difficulties they face, their productivity and efficiency soar to impressive heights. Being away from home compels them to be proactive and resilient.
The nation of Israel faced a similar predicament. Caught between the Red Sea and the pursuing Egyptian army, they seemed unmovable, with no escape in sight. The Egyptian king and his ministers

were livid at the Israelites' newfound freedom and relentlessly pursued them.

At this critical juncture, the Israelites encountered God's intervention. In their desperation, Moses, guided by unwavering faith, struck the sea with his rod. This act symbolized the collective aspirations of a generation that had endured years of suffering in Egypt, tracing back to their forefather Abraham's journey from Ur. Following God's instruction, Moses lifted his rod and stretched out his hand over the sea. Astonishingly, the Red Sea was divided.

What is required of us in such moments is to raise our arms in surrender, embrace courage, and step forward. By doing so, new paths will be unveiled, paving the way for our deliverance. Unfortunately, more often than not, we hesitate to approach our own "Red Seas." We stand at a distance, paralyzed by fear, unwilling to confront the challenges and difficulties that lie ahead.

Instead of remaining stagnant in our comfort zones, we must boldly move closer to the Red Sea. It is there, in the face of adversity, that God stands ready to part the waters and guide us through. We cannot shy away from the tests that life presents; we must gather our strength and confront them head-on.

God's presence accompanies us through the divided Red Sea of our own trials and tribulations. We must have unwavering faith, take decisive steps, and march forward with confidence, knowing that divine guidance is always at hand.

Let us embrace the challenges that lie before us, trusting in God's unfailing support. As we face our personal Red Seas, we will witness the miraculous power that can transform obstacles into opportunities, leading us to new horizons and a brighter future.

In times of crisis, remember that God is near the Red Sea, ready to divide it for our journey. Have faith, step forward, and experience the extraordinary wonders that await us on the other side.

The law of the Lord is perfect, refreshing the soul. The statutes of the Lord are trustworthy, making wise the simple. The precepts of the Lord are right, giving joy to the heart. The commands of the Lord are radiant, giving light to the eyes.

Psalm 19:7-8

9

Your word is a lamp for my feet, a light on my path.
Psalm 119:105

True Blessings

Job's life, overshadowed by deepening crises, also had its moments of materialistic joys. He commanded respect from all quarters, regardless of age or social status. Blessed by God, he devoted himself to helping those in need—the blind, lame, fatherless, widows, and strangers in trouble—while protecting the poor (Job 29:11-16).

Throughout his journey, Job was guided by a divine light. This light was his true blessing, sustaining him through good times and bad. Remarkably, Job never questioned God's intentions, accepting both prosperity and adversity with unwavering faith.

It is common for us to associate material possessions with God's blessings. We believe that more wealth and possessions equate to greater blessings. We measure our prosperity by how smoothly things go in our lives. Conversely, we interpret difficulties and setbacks as signs of a curse. However, we fail to realize that it is often through adversity that God bestows His gifts upon us.

We must understand that wealth, possessions, and power are not true indicators of God's abundant blessings. True blessing lies in the light that illuminates our path. Even in the midst of sorrows, challenges, and darkness, it is this light that uplifts our spirits. This is the essence of Job's words: "When his lamp shone upon my head and by his light I walked through darkness."

Let us not be deceived by the illusion of material prosperity as the sole measure of God's blessings. Instead, let us seek the light that shines within us and guides us through life's trials. It is this light that brings true joy, peace, and fulfillment.

In times of sorrow and despair, remember that the light of God's blessing is always available to us. It is a beacon of hope, leading us out of darkness and into the embrace of divine grace. Embrace the light, and let it illuminate your path as you navigate the challenges of life.

In Christ Jesus, you are all children of God through faith, for all of you who were baptized into Christ have clothed yourselves with Christ. There is neither Jew nor Gentile, neither slave nor free, nor is there male and female, for you are all one in Christ Jesus.

Galatians 3:26-28

10

There are different kinds of gifts, but the same Spirit distributes them. There are different kinds of service, but the same Lord. There are different kinds of working, but in all of them and in everyone, it is the same God at work.

1 Cornthians 12: 4-6

Fullness of Life

God's purpose for us is to experience life in its fullness, allowing every facet of our personality to blossom and bear fruit. We have been abundantly blessed with talents, but are we creating opportunities for our spiritual empowerment and expression? It's not just the responsibility of singers to sing or the duty of pastors to speak from the pulpit. As a community, we can join together in song and prayer. However, in today's world, we often lack the sense of community needed for collective worship, meditation, and fellowship.

With the advent of TV channels and online communities, we can passively listen to choir singing and sermons from the comfort of our homes. We may feel connected through social networking sites, but true spiritual connection and engagement require more than virtual interactions.

Specialization has permeated our lives, even within religious organizations, where singers and choir members are set apart, and priests or preachers solely speak. This principle of division of labor, rooted in industrialization and capitalism, has influenced spiritual enterprises as well.

We must break free from this trend of specialization and division. Singing, sharing our thoughts, praying, and meditating should be embraced by all. It is through building and nurturing communities of like-minded individuals in our neighborhoods that we can fully express our spirituality and radiate its vibrant colors to the world.

Life in its fullness demands the harmonious blending of our skills and talents, allowing them to shine like the colors of a rainbow, ultimately coming together as a brilliant beam of light that brightens our surroundings.

Let us embrace the opportunity to express our spirituality, allowing its diverse colors to flourish and illuminate the world. Together, we can fulfill God's call for a life of abundant fullness.

But our citizenship is in heaven. And we eagerly await a Savior from there, the Lord Jesus Christ, who, by the power that enables him to bring everything under his control, will transform our lowly bodies so that they will be like his glorious body.

Philippians 3:20-21

11

In my Father's house are many rooms; if it were not so, I would have told you. I am going there to prepare a place for you.

John 14: 2-3

Beyond This World

A heartwarming incident involving my young nephew recently sparked a profound contemplation on the concept of life beyond this world. He innocently expressed his regret about forgetting to send a mobile phone with his grandfather before his passing, believing that communication with him would still be possible. This innocent remark holds a deeper truth for Christians - death is not the ultimate end of human life; it is merely a transition.

In Christian faith, we believe that as the physical body ceases to sustain life, the spirit embarks on a journey to its ultimate destination, returning to the original place from which it came. Christ's victory over the powers of darkness and death on the cross assures us that our souls need not be troubled or disturbed any longer.

For those who embrace this belief, our departed loved ones remain a vibrant reality. By living in Christ, we can discern their continued presence, sensing their concerns and thoughts. In my nephew's case, he experiences his grandfather's influence and perceives his presence everywhere. His grandfather is a living reality to him.

Through this child's innocent perspective, we catch a glimpse of the profound Christian understanding of life beyond this world. It may be tempting for some to dismiss it as mere innocence, but it is, in fact, a profound statement of unwavering faith. Death is not the final chapter; it is merely one side of a coin, the gateway to an eternal existence.

As the words of St. John remind us, Jesus Himself proclaimed, "In my Father's house are many rooms; if it were not so, I would have told you. I am going there to prepare a place for you... where I am going." These words offer solace and assurance that there is more to life than meets the eye.

The concept of life beyond this world is not just an abstract belief; it holds significant implications for how we perceive our existence and the purpose of our journey on Earth. It invites us to contemplate our connection to a realm beyond the physical, fostering a deeper understanding of our spiritual nature and the eternal nature of our souls.

In embracing this profound truth, we can find comfort, hope, and a renewed sense of purpose. It ignites a desire within us to live in alignment with the divine, seeking to grow in faith, love, and compassion. By embracing the reality of life beyond this world, we unlock a greater depth of meaning and fulfillment in our present lives.

Let us embrace the profound truth that there is life beyond this world, and allow it to shape our perspectives, actions, and relationships. May it inspire us to live each day with gratitude, purpose, and the assurance that our journey extends far beyond the confines of this earthly existence.

For we are God's handiwork, created in Christ Jesus to do good works, which God prepared in advance for us to do.

Ephesians 2:10

12

But you are a chosen people, a royal priesthood, a holy nation, God's special possession, that you may declare the praises of him who called you out of darkness into his wonderful light.
1 Peter 2:9

Turning Challenges into Opportunities

We have been called as God's chosen people, entrusted with the task of making a difference in the world. Despite the paradoxical nature of the Promised Land, the Israelites redefined the meaning of being chosen through their resilience in the face of adversity. This article explores how God selects individuals to turn challenges into opportunities and highlights the remarkable achievements of Israel in various fields.

The Promised Land, often associated with abundance and prosperity, presented a stark contrast to its literal meaning for the Israelites. Unlike their neighboring nations with rich resources and fertile lands, this region lacked significant natural wealth. One might question the fulfillment of

God's promise as they journeyed through a desert plagued by constant strife. Nevertheless, the Israelites embraced their role as God's chosen people and transformed their challenging circumstances into opportunities for growth.

Israel's journey exemplifies the transformation of adversity into success. Despite the initial limitations of their land, they emerged as global leaders in bio-technology, agriculture, and farm technologies. Through their advancements, Israel offers a beacon of hope for a world striving for food security. Even in the face of unfavorable conditions, such as heat, humidity, and limited resources, they made remarkable achievements in the dairy industry, showcasing their determination and resilience. Moreover, Israel's focus on rural poverty eradication through Small and Micro Enterprises (SMEs) and cooperative organizational frameworks demonstrates their commitment to egalitarian-oriented development. These accomplishments serve as a testament to their ability to overcome challenges and create a positive impact.

The achievements of Israel extend beyond technological advancements. Despite a war-like atmosphere, there exists a profound sense of Shalom, or peace. Their story serves as a powerful reminder that we often overlook the potentials bestowed upon us. Instead of blaming external factors for our plight, we must embrace the realization that

God has chosen us to make a difference wherever we are placed.

God calls upon His chosen people to rise to the challenge of making a difference in the world. The Israelites' journey to the Promised Land exemplifies the transformation of adversity into opportunity. Despite initial hardships, they emerged as leaders in various fields, offering solutions to global challenges. The story of Israel serves as an eye-opener, reminding us that we, too, are chosen by God. Embracing this calling requires commitment, sacrifice, and perseverance, as the journey to fulfilling our purpose may not always be smooth. Let us rise to the challenge and make a lasting impact, following in the footsteps of those who have gone before us.

Finally, brothers and sisters, whatever is true, whatever is noble, whatever is right, whatever is pure, whatever is lovely, whatever is admirable—if anything is excellent or praiseworthy—think about such things.

Philippians 4:8

13

Overcoming Negativity

Anxiety weighs down the heart, but a kind word cheers it up.

Proverbs 12:25

When seeking advice or suggestions from others, we often encounter two distinct types of responses: those that discourage and those that encourage. This applies to various fields, such as medical, legal, or financial consultations.

The impact of these interactions can significantly affect our mindset and overall well-being. While some individuals radiate positivity and instill confidence, others inadvertently convey negative vibes, leading to disappointment and worry. However, it is crucial to recognize the role of God's Spirit in uplifting and strengthening us, ensuring that we do not succumb to the traps of discouragement and negativity.

Approaching professionals for guidance in areas like healthcare or finance can elicit a range of responses. Positive-minded individuals have the ability to make even daunting tasks seem manageable. They instill a sense of ease and assurance, assuring us that things will work out.

On the other hand, some individuals may unknowingly project negativity, leaving us feeling disheartened and depressed. The reasons behind their discouragement can vary, from intentionally delaying assistance to lacking up-to-date knowledge in their field.

It is essential for us to recognize the impact we have on others when they approach us for help. Discouraging and causing disgust in others is the work of the devil. In contrast, the Holy Spirit never seeks to discourage us but rather strengthens and uplifts our spirits. By resisting the devil's influence and embracing the guidance of God's Spirit, we can avoid falling into the trap of negativity and discouragement.

It is important for us to remember that the Holy Spirit never seeks to discourage but rather strengthens and empowers us. We should be mindful of the impact our words and actions have on others, striving to be a source of encouragement rather than discouragement. By resisting the devil's attempts to bring negativity into our lives, we can remain steadfast in the uplifting power of God's Spirit. Let us embrace this strength and radiate positivity to make a positive difference in the lives of others.

Arise, shine, for your light has come, and the glory of the Lord rises upon you.

Isaiah 60:1

14

Arise, shine, for your light has come, and the glory of the Lord rises upon you.
Isaih: 60:1

Arise and Shine

In moments of despair and hopelessness, when the challenges of life seem insurmountable, we often find ourselves engulfed in negative thoughts. The weight of burdens and the grief of loss can cast a shadow over our spirits.

However, amidst the darkness, there is a divine call beckoning us to rise and shine, for the glory of the Lord is upon us. Just as sunbeams illuminate the grass and wildflowers, we too are called to be a source of light and hope in the situations we find ourselves in.

One particular morning, I woke up feeling despondent, as if the world was conspiring against me. The weight of past difficulties and the recent loss of my father due to a prolonged illness only added to my despair. Negative thoughts consumed me, leaving me feeling hopeless and helpless. However, as I walked in my garden, I witnessed a captivating sight: sunbeams delicately caressing the grass and wildflowers, casting a radiant glow upon them.

In that moment, the beauty of nature reminded me of the words spoken by the prophet Isaiah: "Arise and shine like the sun; the glory of the Lord is shining on you." It was a profound realization that I still had a journey ahead of me, and God expected me to be a beacon of light to others wherever I found myself.

With this newfound clarity, my negative thoughts dissipated. I recognized that God had entrusted each of us with a mission to illuminate the situations in which we are placed. Despite the challenges and uncertainties, we are called to rise above despair and shine with the radiance of God's glory. Our purpose is to bring hope, encouragement, and positivity to those around us, serving as a guiding light in their lives.

when we find ourselves overwhelmed by the trials and tribulations of life, it is essential to remember our divine calling to arise and shine. Just as the sun's rays illuminate the world, we are entrusted with the task of bringing light to the situations we encounter. Despite the darkness that may surround us, we have the power to dispel negativity and offer hope. Embracing this calling allows us to live purposefully, fulfilling God's plan for our lives and becoming agents of change in a world that needs illumination. Let us rise, shine, and reflect the glory of the Lord, spreading light and hope to all those we encounter on our journey.

For my thoughts are not your thoughts, neither are your ways my ways," declares the Lord. "As the heavens are higher than the earth, so are my ways higher than your ways and my thoughts than your thoughts.

Isaiah 55:8-9

15

Commit to the LORD whatever you do, and he will establish your plans.

Proverbs 16:3

Embracing God's Ways

In the journey of life, Christians are called to be industrious and dedicated, fulfilling their responsibilities and tasks to the best of their abilities. However, there are moments when our efforts seem fruitless, and we question the purpose of our actions. It is during such times that we are reminded of the profound truth expressed in Isaiah 55:8-9:

"For my thoughts are not your thoughts, nor are your ways my ways, says the Lord. For as the heavens are higher than the earth, so are my ways higher than your ways, and my thoughts than your thoughts."Often, we find ourselves uncertain if our actions align with the Lord's will. We may face situations where our long-term plans lack financial success or overlook important considerations, leading us into trouble. However, it is crucial to recognize that God may have different plans and purposes for us, beyond immediate financial gain. We must trust in His wisdom and guidance, knowing that His ways are higher and His thoughts are greater than ours.

Unexpected events and circumstances can disrupt our lives, leaving us bewildered and questioning their purpose. These experiences, although challenging, serve as opportunities for God to refine us, strengthen us, and mold us into the individuals that He desires us to be. Jesus Christ calls us to strive for perfection, to deliver our very best in all aspects of life. While society often measures success by material wealth and possessions, true prosperity extends to the spiritual realms.

The ups and downs, crises, and uncertainties we encounter hold a clear purpose in God's plan for our lives. He uses these experiences to sharpen our character, strengthen our faith, and build our resilience.

Just as an entrepreneur meticulously reviews and adjusts their business plan, God evaluates and refines us through short-term and medium-term assessments. He guides us, molding us into individuals capable of navigating life independently.

Embracing God's ways requires trust and faith in His divine wisdom. While our human understanding may be limited, His ways surpass our comprehension.

We must not solely pursue worldly prosperity but seek spiritual prosperity, aligning ourselves with God's greater purpose for our lives. In the face of life's uncertainties and challenges, we can find solace and strength in knowing that God uses these circumstances to shape us, refine us, and ultimately lead us toward His desired perfection. Let us surrender our plans and desires to Him, embracing His higher ways, and trusting that His thoughts and ways are far beyond our own.

Trust in the Lord with all your heart and lean not on your own understanding; in all your ways submit to him, and he will make your paths straight.
Proverbs 3:5-6

16

So do not fear, for I am with you; do not be dismayed, for I am your God. I will strengthen you and help you; I will uphold you with my righteous right hand.
Isaiah 41:10

Seeking God's Guidance

In our journey to fulfill the tasks and responsibilities assigned to us by God, we may face external circumstances and discouraging words that tempt us to withdraw. However, it is during these moments that we must remember the importance of persevering and completing the work set before us, regardless of the outcome. Let us trust in God's guidance and not be deterred by temporary setbacks or negative reviews.

Withdrawing from an activity midway should be avoided, even if the results don't meet our initial expectations. We should not allow discouragement to hinder our progress. Instead, we must press forward and fulfill our duties and responsibilities faithfully, trusting that God is with us every step of the way.

While seeking advice from experts and listening to different opinions is valuable, our ultimate consultant should be God Himself. Our prayer time becomes our consulting time, where we seek divine guidance and align our decisions with His will. It is essential to carefully assess the suggestions and opinions we receive, recognizing that not all advice may be beneficial. The Holy Spirit, as our helper, empowers us to discern what is good for us and what may lead us astray.

It is crucial to be cautious when selecting advisors and mentors. Surrounding ourselves with individuals who lack expertise or resources in the areas we seek guidance can easily lead to misguided decisions and troubles. We should seek the counsel of those who are knowledgeable and experienced in the relevant fields.

There may be times when we find ourselves without access to reliable advisors or mentors, feeling isolated and uncertain. During such periods, we can turn to God, prayer, and the reading of the Bible for solace and direction. God becomes our friend, supporter, guide, and mentor in our moments of loneliness. His presence becomes evident in our workplaces, in unfamiliar surroundings, and wherever we need Him. As we navigate through life's challenges, let us make God our ultimate advisor. Rather than being discouraged by external circumstances or negative reviews, we must remain steadfast and committed to fulfilling our tasks and responsibilities. Seeking guidance through prayer and the Holy Spirit's assistance, we can discern the right path and make wise decisions. Even in times of isolation and loneliness, God's presence becomes our strength and source of guidance. Let us trust in Him, knowing that He will be our unfailing friend, supporter, guide, and mentor throughout our journey.

Trust in the Lord and do good; dwell in the land and enjoy safe pasture. Take delight in the Lord, and he will give you the desires of your heart. Commit your way to the Lord; trust in him and he will do this.

Psalm 37:3-5

17

My sheep listen to my voice; I know them,
and they follow me.
John 10:27

Unleashing Our Potentials

In the Gospel of John, we find a powerful message that holds universal relevance: Jesus instructs the disciples to cast their nets on the right side of the boat, resulting in an abundant catch of fish.

This story reminds us that God's intervention and direction can make a significant difference in our lives. It teaches us the importance of recognizing His presence and listening to His guidance.

Often, we find ourselves toiling and striving without seeing the desired results. Frustration sets in, and we question why our efforts seem in vain. However, amidst our struggles, we may have neglected to seek God's direction or to listen attentively to His voice. Like the disciples after the resurrection, we may be uncertain about the path we should take.

In the story, the disciples, including Peter, decide to go fishing. They spend the entire night without catching anything. It is at this moment, early in the morning, that Jesus appears on the shore, although the disciples initially do not recognize Him. Similarly, Jesus is constantly present in our lives, offering guidance and direction, but we often fail to recognize His voice or ignore His presence.

This story imparts two essential messages to us: firstly, we need to be attuned to recognizing Jesus' presence in our lives, and secondly, we must actively listen to His directions. When we do so, we will experience abundant blessings, peace, and happiness. Our talents, skills, and lives will find meaning and fulfillment.

In a previous encounter recorded in Luke 5:4, Jesus tells Simon Peter to cast the nets into deep water for a catch. When they obeyed His command, they caught such an overwhelming number of fish that their nets began to break. This account highlights the necessity of listening to Jesus' voice. God has bestowed each of us with unique talents, skills, and knowledge, and our potentials are immeasurable. However, we often hesitate to explore and utilize these gifts fully. We need Jesus' guidance to identify our skills and talents and to direct them in the right path. He knows where and how to fish, and by listening to Him, our potentials can be unleashed and flourish. Let us open our hearts to Jesus, inviting Him to intervene in our lives, so that we may discover our purpose and make a meaningful impact in the world.

Recognizing the presence of Jesus in our lives and listening to His voice are pivotal in unleashing our potentials and finding fulfillment. Like the disciples who cast their nets on the right side of the boat, resulting in an abundant catch, we too can experience the blessings and joy that come from aligning our lives with God's guidance. Let us seek His direction, trust in His plans, and allow Him to unleash our talents and skills for His glory.

You make known to me the path of life; you will fill me with joy in your presence, with eternal pleasures at your right hand.

Psalm 16:11

18

Take delight in the LORD, and he will give you the desires of your heart.

Psalm 37:4

Receiving True Blessings

In today's world, the concept of being blessed is often associated with wealth, power, and fame. However, the biblical understanding of blessings is quite different. Jesus' teachings in the Sermon on the Mount remind us that true blessedness comes from a different perspective. It is not about material possessions or worldly achievements but about the state of our hearts and our surrender to the almighty. Let us explore the true meaning of blessings and the significance of surrendering to God.

In Matthew 5:3-8, Jesus shares the Beatitudes, revealing the qualities that lead to blessedness. He declares the blessedness of the poor in spirit, the meek, those who mourn, the merciful, the peacemakers, the pure in heart, and those who hunger

and thirst for righteousness. These individuals, with their humble and righteous attitudes, will receive the blessings of heaven. The kingdom of heaven is promised to them.
Contrary to popular beliefs that equate blessings with luck or material wealth, Jesus emphasizes the importance of inner qualities and attitudes. Being blessed is not about accumulating possessions or outshining others; it is about aligning our hearts with God's will and experiencing His peace and happiness.

To understand the true nature of blessings, we need to reprogram our thoughts and refer to the fundamental teachings of holy books and religions. Jesus invites us to make ultimate sacrifices for the sake of righteousness, justice, and peace. The meek, the peacemakers, and those who stand for justice will be called children of God. However, embracing this call comes with risks, as peacemaking may require standing up for justice, even at the cost of personal safety.

It is essential to recognize that being blessed has no connection to luck or material possessions. True happiness and blessedness are found in a state of mind that comes from surrendering completely to the almighty. As the Bhagavad Gita teaches, complete surrender to God is the path to receiving peace and happiness.

Wealth and material possessions do not guarantee lasting happiness. Only when we surrender ourselves to God, acknowledging His sovereignty over our lives, can we experience true blessings. Surrendering to God means letting go of our selfish desires and seeking His will above all else. It is through this surrender that we find true peace, contentment, and a deep sense of fulfillment.

In a world that often equates blessings with material wealth and external achievements, it is vital to rediscover the true meaning of being blessed. Jesus' teachings remind us that blessedness comes from a humble and righteous heart, from being poor in spirit and pure in heart. Surrendering to God and aligning our lives with His will lead us to experience the blessings of heaven.

Let us reprogram our thoughts and beliefs, seeking to understand the fundamental teachings of holy books and religions. By surrendering to the almighty, we open ourselves to His peace and happiness, transcending the temporary and fleeting pleasures of the world. May we surrender ourselves completely to God and receive His abundant blessings in our lives.

Do not conform to the pattern of this world, but be transformed by the renewing of your mind. Then you will be able to test and approve what God's will is—his good, pleasing and perfect will.

Romans 12:2

TDW Productions & Publishing

TDW Productions & Publishing is a dynamic and empowering digital publishing and communication hub dedicated to helping writers and authors thrive, express themselves, and make their mark in the literary world. At TDW, we believe in the power of storytelling and aim to provide a platform where creativity knows no bounds.

Our mission is to unearth the next big ideas and breathe life into them through various forms of publication. From books and reports to both fiction and non-fiction works, we curate a diverse collection that captivates readers from all walks of life.

At TDW's we extend our expertise to a wide array of projects and collaborate to produce compelling content, documentaries and scripts tailored for different mediums and channels. We craft narratives that leave a lasting impact.

Beyond publication, TDW ventures into the realm of media and communication campaigns, helping brands flourish in the digital landscape. We undertake brand development and promotion exercises, ensuring that each client's message is communicated effectively and resonates with their target audience. Our specialized and focused campaigns have delivered remarkable results for diverse clients, amplifying their reach and influence.

At TDW, we're not just a publishing house; we are a creative powerhouse committed to empowering writers, authors, and clients alike. We believe in the transformative power of words and storytelling, and our passion for creativity drives us to explore new frontiers, making a real difference in the world of digital content.

So, whether you're an aspiring writer seeking a platform to shine or a brand looking to leave a lasting impression, TDW is here to bring your vision to life and make it thrive in the digital realm. Join us on this exciting journey of creativity, expression, and boundless possibilities. Together, we'll craft a narrative that captures hearts, sparks imagination, and leaves a legacy for generations to come. Welcome to TDW, where your stories become unforgettable realities.

To become a published author or to contribute to our various publications, please get in touch with us at:

Email: thedigitalwordhub@gmail.com
https://tdwpublishing.com/

www.ingramcontent.com/pod-product-compliance
Lightning Source LLC
Chambersburg PA
CBHW050024170726
48282CB00025B/530
* 9 7 8 9 3 9 1 8 2 8 4 4 8 *